# THE
# WRITING SKILLS
# POCKETBOOK

## By Stella Collins & Beth Curl

*Drawings by Phil Hailstone*

"Delightfully clear! Writing a book about writing is brave – and this one follows its own advice to the letter."
**Dr. Peter Honey, Occupational Psychologist and Management Trainer**

"It's obvious from reading this book that Stella Collins & Beth Curl know exactly what they are talking about. It's a marvelously clear, concise, and compelling treatment."
Robert B. Cialdini, Author of Influence: Science and Practice

*Published by:*
**Management Pocketbooks Ltd**
Laurel House, Station Approach, Alresford, Hants SO24 9JH, U.K.
Tel: +44 (0)1962 735573   Fax: +44 (0)1962 733637
Email: sales@pocketbook.co.uk
Website: www.pocketbook.co.uk

© Stella Collins & Beth Curl 2012

This edition published 2012   ISBN 978 1 906610 45 6

E-book ISBN: 978 1 908284 26 6

British Library Cataloguing-in-Publication Data – A catalogue record for this book is available
from the British Library.

Design, typesetting and graphics by **efex ltd**.   Printed in U.K.

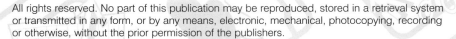

# CONTENTS

4

# INTRODUCTION:
## Writing in the Real World

## INTRODUCTION: WRITING IN THE REAL WORLD

# WHY SHOULD YOU READ THIS BOOK?

You probably spend some of your time at work writing; most people write multiple emails and short communications and a smaller number of large but significantly time consuming documents. By implementing the hints and tips in this book you will reduce the time you spend writing, editing and rewriting.

Whenever you set pen to paper (or more likely fingers to the keyboard) you're communicating. What you write affects what other people think about you, how they judge you, how they feel and what they may do. Writing well helps you create the right impression and communicate the tone and content of your message clearly.

This book is about writing in a work context so we'll refer to emails, reports, instructions and other business documents. What you learn can be applied to all types of writing, but we won't cover writing you might do for pleasure (so no poetry or love letters).

You'll find some basics of punctuation and grammar and suggestions for further reading. We'll give you a process and structure to make your written communications more effective, and hints and tips that make a difference to you and your readers.

# INTRODUCTION: WRITING IN THE REAL WORLD

## THE CHALLENGE OF INFORMATION OVERLOAD

We were promised a paperless office but instead got information overload. Instead of writing less, we have to read and write more. So, how can you make sure your writing gets read when there's so much competition for your readers' attention? And how can you make writing quicker, easier and less work for you?

This Pocketbook is about building effective writing skills for busy people in business.

It will help you:
- With an easy three phase approach to writing
- Simplify your writing so people get the information they need
- Choose the right style for communicating with your readers
- With tips, techniques and practical experience drawn from real life

The book gives you a toolkit to convey your message unambiguously, concisely and quickly.

# BARRIERS TO WRITING & READING

Most people aren't trained writers – you've got a core job to do and writing is merely incidental, something you're expected to do as part of your job.

Possibly the last time you got any help with writing was at school or university, where your aim was to impress people with your knowledge and intellect; but business writing has a different purpose – it is mainly about sharing information.

Writing is a reduced form of communication – you have to supply enough information without overwhelming readers with detail. And you have to get the tone right without anyone seeing your gestures or hearing your tone of voice.

Readers are busy people too. Your new operating manual requires their attention at the same time as emails, phone calls and meetings – how will you ensure your written communication gets read and actioned before they get distracted?

# WHAT WILL HELP YOU IMPROVE YOUR WRITING?

When we deliver writing skills courses, the most common questions we are asked about writing are:

- ☐ How do I get started?
- ☐ How can I be more concise?
- ☐ How do I summarise information without losing detail?
- ☐ How can I write quicker?
- ☐ What's the best way to adapt my style to different audiences?
- ☐ How can I make sure I get my message across distinctly?
- ☐ How do I organise my information and not get bogged down in detail?
- ☐ How can I avoid constantly rewriting?
- ☐ Is there a better way to plan than 'splurge and edit?'
- ☐ What do I do when my boss changes it and then their boss changes it back?

Tick those that apply to you and then add your own questions or challenges.

# OVERVIEW OF CONTENT

The solution we propose will help you with all these challenges. First you'll encounter a three stage process:

**Phase 1: Before Starting to Write**
**Phase 2: Writing Clearly & Concisely**
**Phase 3: Reviewing and Polishing**

You can use this process for anything you need to write in the business environment: emails, notes, reports, proposals, instructions, letters, etc. When you're faced with a blank page, or screen, and a request to write something, this well-tested process makes writing easier, faster and less daunting.

Then you'll discover some of the more subtle aspects of written communication in the chapter **Getting the Tone Right** – how to have impact and communicate clearly, how to set the appropriate tone for different audiences and how to be more persuasive.

The final chapter is dedicated to **HITs: Hints, Ideas and Tips** to make sure your documents get read and your messages are understood and acted on.

 On the next page you will find a map to help you navigate around the book.

## INTRODUCTION: WRITING IN THE REAL WORLD

# NAVIGATING AROUND THE BOOK

**PHASE 1**

**PHASE 2**

**PHASE 3**

# YOUR PERSONAL CHALLENGES

*intro*

What aspects of writing do you find difficult?

........................................................................

........................................................................

........................................................................

What would you like to improve in your writing?

........................................................................

........................................................................

........................................................................

**PHASE 1**

**Before Starting to Write**
- What is my purpose?
- Who are my readers?
- Planning the content and structure
- Testing the plan

## PHASE 1: BEFORE STARTING TO WRITE

# WHAT IS MY PURPOSE?

How often do you send an email, write a quick report or briefing for someone, or write to a client or customer to explain, apologise or to persuade them?

Do you ever find yourself staring at a blank page wondering, how to start? Or find you've written dozens of pages but aren't sure what needs to be edited out?

Before you start to write anything the first question to ask yourself is, *'what is the purpose of my writing?'*

You are highly unlikely to have the luxury of spending all day uninterrupted when you have a lengthy document to write. It's more likely that you will face frequent interruptions and distractions. When you have a clear purpose written down, it's much easier to return to your document, refocus your thoughts and continue writing.

So is your purpose in writing your document to inform, persuade, enquire, explain, confirm, instruct or build relationships? What other purposes do you have?

# WHAT IS MY PURPOSE?

These are some of the purposes people may have when they start writing:

- **Inform** – you need to write a notice and an email to tell people that the canteen will be closed for maintenance next week
- **Persuade** – you want your boss to let you attend a conference that she normally goes to, but she's out of the office this week so you can only communicate by email
- **Enquire** – you want to know whether the information you're waiting for will be ready in time for you to add it to your proposal
- **Explain** – you need to write a short report to explain why you took a particular decision
- **Confirm** – you are arranging a senior management meeting and need to make sure the venue knows dates, numbers and lunch arrangements
- **Instruct** – someone new has joined the team and it's your job to make sure they have instructions for all the systems they'll use
- **Build relationships** – you know you're going to have to work closely with someone in a different location and want to start off on a good footing

# WHAT IS MY PURPOSE?

When you know what your purpose is, writing becomes easier because you know what key messages you need to focus on. Once you have identified your purpose, what you write will be more obvious to your reader and your message is more likely to be read and acted upon.

Writing a **statement of purpose** gives you a clear idea of what you want to write, how you want to write and what you want people actually to do after they've read it.

EXAMPLE

*To inform staff about the new flexi-working scheme and to explain how to enrol on the new system by 20 December.*

EXAMPLE

*To write an email to persuade our most valued customers to complete an online survey about our key product lines, including a testimonial, before the end of the month.*

A statement of purpose has three parts: what I want to achieve, what I want the reader to do, and when.

## PHASE 1: BEFORE STARTING TO WRITE

# WHAT IS MY PURPOSE?

Now decide your statement of purpose for the next document you need to write. Even a quick email needs to have a clear purpose.

I want to...

I want the reader to....

When...          (insert date)

If someone else has asked you to write something and you're not sure of their purpose, then you need to go back to them and ask them to clarify it. Don't start writing until you are both sure of the objective and scope of the communication.

## PHASE 1: BEFORE STARTING TO WRITE

# WHO ARE MY READERS?

Having decided what your purpose is, you now need to identify your reader. Who are you writing the document for? The more you know about your readers, the more effectively you will be able to focus and organise your writing.

Whatever you are writing you need to think about who's going to read it. Sometimes you will know the reader personally which makes it easier to answer these questions, but often you may have to guess or make some assumptions to make sure you write appropriately to them.

How senior are they compared to you? How formal do you need to be? What's their educational level, what's their background knowledge of the subject?

What mood might they be in when they read your document? What's the psychological impact on them? (We'll consider this in more detail in the chapter: Getting the tone right).

# WHO ARE MY READERS?

Ask yourself questions such as:

- What do they need to know – what is of real interest to them? You don't need to tell them everything you know
- How will they use this information? Will they need to re-use the information in a presentation or simply do what you've asked?
- What are their attitudes to the information and to me? Is it vital information they've been waiting for and you're the expert, or are you unknown to them and it's the first time you're approaching them?
- What impact will your writing have on them? Will it affect their career or just change where you go for lunch?
- Where will they read the information – on screen, on a phone, on paper? This will affect how much you can present to them
- When is a good time for them to receive this information – are they right in the middle of an important project and your document will be a distraction or are they urgently waiting for it?

# WHO ARE MY READERS?

List all the potential readers for your document, what you know about them and what they will want to get from reading it.

For instance, for a report on the project you've just completed your readers may be:

- Another colleague – who wants to know the methodology, how to repeat the work, detailed results and conclusions
- Your manager – who needs a record of the work in order to check its validity and to plan similar future projects
- The Managing Director – who only wants a brief summary of what was done, results, conclusions and recommendations

You'll have to organise the text to offer a range of reading strategies so the different readers can find what they need (we'll come to planning next).

Or you might simply be writing an email to a group of colleagues to arrange a date for a meeting and the readers are all of a similar status and doing the same job. You will need to make the arrangements clear but everyone is likely to need similar information.

# WHO ARE MY READERS?

Your readership and impact may be wider than you think if the text is passed on.

An email can be forwarded to people you had not imagined would read it. If you've written a very informal email to a colleague using slang and omitting punctuation, do you really want that passed onto a senior manager or a customer?

Written documents can be legally binding (legal cases are now coming up where even twitter and facebook comments have been used as evidence) so you need to consider what you write and how it will be interpreted.

Reports may stay in the system for a long time but people may still have to act on your recommendations so they need to have enough information to adequately understand your recommendations or decision making at the time.

You are an ambassador for your organisation and can create your own reputation!

## PHASE 1: BEFORE STARTING TO WRITE

# PLANNING THE CONTENT & STRUCTURE

You are now clear about your purpose and your readers, so next you can plan the content and the structure for your document.

Taking time to plan before you start to write:

- Makes the writing process easier and quicker
- Saves you time in writing and editing
- Reduces queries and corrections
- Helps you write a document that gets your message across and has the desired impact on your readers
- Gives you something to test before you start the main work of 'writing'

Even small pieces of writing, like emails, benefit from planning; if you jot down your thoughts before you start to write, you will quickly construct a coherent message.

*'To fail to plan is to plan to fail.'*

We will introduce you to several planning methods – try them all out and see what suits you best!

# PLANNING WITH MIND MAPS

One of our favourite methods of planning is to use mind maps.

The term *mind map* was coined by Tony Buzan, who did a great deal of research into their efficacy, but visual plans have been used for centuries for brainstorming, thinking, problem solving and learning. They are also called webs, spider diagrams, spray diagrams, brain maps and cognitive cartographs, amongst others!

Previous mind mappers include Porphyry of Tyros (3rd century philosopher), Ramon Llull (a 13th century writer and philosopher), Leonardo da Vinci and even Charles Darwin.

Mind maps use colour, images, structure as well as key words and can be computerised or hand drawn. Type *mind map* into a search engine and you will find lots of options.

# PLANNING WITH MIND MAPS

Kipling's list of six questions forms the basis of most good plans and we have used a simple mind map to display them.

'I keep six honest serving-men
(They taught me all I knew); Their
names are What and Why and When
And How and Where and Who.'
**Rudyard Kipling**

# PLANNING WITH MIND MAPS

If you were writing an important email to organise a site visit, you could start by capturing all your ideas as a mind map and then ordering them. When you start writing you can use the mindmap as a checklist to make sure you have covered everything. You might decide to put the detail in a separate document and only list the key points in the email.

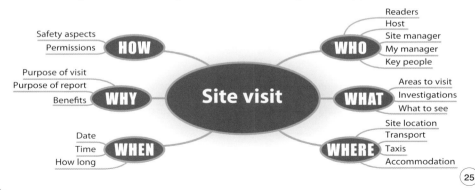

**Site visit**

HOW
- Safety aspects
- Permissions

WHY
- Purpose of visit
- Purpose of report
- Benefits

WHEN
- Date
- Time
- How long

WHO
- Readers
- Host
- Site manager
- My manager
- Key people

WHAT
- Areas to visit
- Investigations
- What to see

WHERE
- Site location
- Transport
- Taxis
- Accommodation

## PHASE 1: BEFORE STARTING TO WRITE

# PLANNING WITH POST-ITS

Post-it notes provide another excellent method of planning.

Brain storm all the ideas you want to include in your document and write each one on a post-it. Allow your mind to range freely – just capture all the thoughts for now.

Once you have got all your ideas, group them into a suitable structure for your document. The advantages of post-it planning are that you can easily add more ideas, move post-its and group them in different ways.

If you are planning with another person, record all your ideas separately first and then you can enjoy the discussion and evaluation together. It provides a physical and visual method of planning, generates more ideas than you can do individually and is fun too!

Take a digital photograph of your plan – it's an easy way to keep a record.

# STRUCTURING YOUR DOCUMENT

The structure of your document is like a skeleton or framework – it holds it together and guides readers through to find the information they need.

A document with no structure is just a heap of text, with no organisation of thought. People have to read the whole text to understand the message; there are no short cuts to help them find key information or interpret it.

After creating a plan of your content, the next step is to provide a structure. Group information into related chunks and choose an order; this will be determined by the purpose of your document and your readers' needs.

# STRUCTURING YOUR DOCUMENT

## EXAMPLE

When we wrote this book we started with a huge mind map of all the topics we wished to cover. By thinking about our purpose, our audience and our content we began to find a structure to serve all those needs.

We decided the book could be organised into a five part structure and we arranged the topics under those five chapters.

Then we created the navigational map of the book to provide a visual way of finding the parts of the book that are of interest to individual readers or for anyone wanting to find a particular topic again.

By repeating the navigational map at the start of each chapter, we help readers quickly identify where they are in the whole process, and see the detailed contents of that particular chapter.

# STRUCTURE: KEY MESSAGE FIRST

In this information rich world, you are overloaded with data and written communication and so probably do not read everything you receive – which makes you very similar to everyone else. You may read just the first few lines or skim read for the important facts. It is very easy to overlook an important detail when it is buried in the text.

Make your key messages obvious to your reader by putting key information first!

# STRUCTURE: KEY MESSAGE FIRST

You use this principle when you:

- Use informative titles
- Give an executive summary
- Tell the reader the key topic in the first sentence
- Ask for what you want in the first line
- Use headlines to highlight key information

Whenever you read or hear new information, your brain checks to see if you know anything about that topic already; relating the new information to what you know enables you to receive, interpret and understand new information more effectively. So by giving key information first, you allow your readers to tune in more quickly to your message.

# STRUCTURE: USE SIGNPOSTS

Readers can navigate easily around a well-structured written communication and zoom in on the information they need without reading the whole text.

You have a range of structural devices at your disposal to make the structure obvious to the reader. They act as navigational aids and signposts for the reader:

- Headings
- Summary
- Title
- Contents page
- Index
- Sections
- Headings and sub-headings

- Bullet Points
- Numbering
- White space
- Fonts – type and size
- Bold
- Colour
- Layout

Even a letter or an email is easier to read when headings and other structural devices are used to lead the eye around the page.

# EXAMPLE STRUCTURES: INSTRUCTIONS

If you were asked to write instructions for using a piece of equipment, a good structure would be:

- Title
- Brief overview
- Aims and objectives
- Cautions, warnings and risks
- Step by step numbered instructions with illustrations
- Frequently asked questions
- Trouble shooting

# EXAMPLE STRUCTURES: INVESTIGATING & REPORTING BACK

Imagine your boss has asked you to find out about something and then to report back. For a simple matter an email may be appropriate; for something more complex, a Word document would be better and a suitable structure could be:

- Title
- Summary
- Contents list/page
- Introduction including background, aims and objectives
- Methods
- Results
- Discussion
- Conclusion
- Appendices for detailed supporting information

# EXAMPLE STRUCTURES: PERSUASIVE PROPOSAL

With a persuasive proposal, your task is to lead your readers to the conclusion or decision that you think is a win-win. Present your strongest options first and then the less favoured alternatives.

- Introduction, background, situation, objectives, context – not everybody will already have this information
- Criteria for the preferred solution including your 'authority' for making the recommendation
- Method of evaluating the evidence
- Where relevant, point out actions already taken in making progress compatible with your recommendation
- Present your best option first – point out the benefits and also potential losses if the best option isn't chosen
- Then present alternatives, which are still satisfactory
- Describe easy-to-implement next steps to make the recommendation happen

# EXAMPLE STRUCTURES: BUSINESS REPORT

- Title, author, date
- Contents
- Executive summary
- Introduction and terms of reference (or aims/scope)
- Background/ history/ situation
- Methodology
- Issues/ implications/ opportunities/ threats, with source-referenced facts, figures and evidence

- Solution/ action/ decision options with inputs and outputs, implications and results
- Recommendations and actions with input and outcomes costs, and return on investment
- Appendices
- Optional bibliography and acknowledgements

(Not every report will need this level of complexity.)

An executive summary must be concise, include key issues, options and recommendations and never be more than two pages.

# TESTING THE PLAN

Testing the plan is a crucial step in this first phase, particularly if you are writing a large document. This can save a lot of time and anguish later.

Even short documents such as letters and emails may need testing if they are particularly important to you, will have a big impact on the recipient or if they are to be re-used many times. It's probably easier to do this with a quick draft rather than a full plan.

Get a second opinion on your plan and structure of your document with the commissioning manager, editor, or client to ensure it meets their expectations, before you begin the process of writing. Other people may notice things you've missed, or can see alternative interpretations or implications to those you intended.

If there have been any misunderstandings or changes in circumstances you have time to agree alterations while still at the planning stage. Managers can see that work is progressing and it demonstrates your organised approach, adding to your credibility.

**Writing Clearly & Concisely**
- Simple style
- Take care with jargon and technical terms
- Remove redundant words and phrases
- Sentence length
- Signpost words
- Main point first in sentences
- Active versus passive voice
- Make written communication personal
- Paragraphs
- Punctuation
- Layout
- Illustrations, tables and graphs
- Summaries

**PHASE 2**

# SIMPLE STYLE TO EXPRESS COMPLEX IDEAS

In business you need to communicate efficiently so your reader gets the message with least effort in the shortest time. Your style of writing affects how easily people read, understand and accept your message.

When you read you are using your working memory, which has only a limited capacity and gets quickly overloaded. When you use simple words, sentences and structures, readers experience a feeling of 'cognitive ease' – it is straightforward to process what you have written and they are more likely to continue reading. And research indicates that you will seem to be more organised and more intelligent. This is even more important when your ideas are complex.

Don't bury your beautiful, intricate ideas in long, wordy sentences – let the ideas shine out!

# SIMPLE STYLE TO EXPRESS COMPLEX IDEAS

Here are eight easy rules to make your writing a pleasure to read:

1. Take care with jargon.
2. Use simple words.
3. Write short sentences.
4. Remove redundant words and phrases.
5. Write active rather than passive sentences.
6. Use verbs and not nominalisations.
7. Use the personal rather than impersonal.
8. Avoid long noun compounds – 'honeybee inspired visual control strategies'.

# TAKE CARE WITH JARGON & TECHNICAL WORDS

Specialist and technical terms are essential verbal shorthand and need to be used where appropriate. Knowing the jargon makes people feel they belong to the group and helps to establish group identity, but it also excludes outsiders and newcomers and hinders communication between different groups. When you use jargon that people don't understand, you are effectively saying:

*'I don't care if you don't understand me, because you're not part of my group.'*

To avoid problems with jargon:

- Use general terms as much as possible
- Give clear definitions for technical terms
- Provide a glossary
- Keep jargon out of the parts of the document that most people will read

What jargon do you use? Is it appropriate in every document you write – do all your readers understand it?

# USE SIMPLE WORDS

This is a list of common phrases that can easily be simplified

| Instead of: | Use: | Instead of: | Use: |
|---|---|---|---|
| At the present moment in time | Now | In the majority of cases | Usually/ Mostly |
| Due to the fact that | Because | Pertaining to | About |
| Is equipped with | Has | Subsequent to | After |
| Is provided with | Has | Foreign imports | Imports |
| In conjunction with | With | Joint agreement | Agreement |
| Throughout the entire | Throughout | Consensus of opinion | Consensus |
| Final result | Result | In the course of | During |
| In close proximity to | Near | As a consequence of | Because |

# REMOVE REDUNDANT WORDS & PHRASES

Some phrases don't add anything to your writing and are just padding! Leave them out unless you can think of a good reason to include them.

You will see people write these phrases when they haven't got very much to say or want to avoid committing themselves.

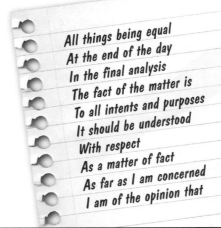

All things being equal
At the end of the day
In the final analysis
The fact of the matter is
To all intents and purposes
It should be understood
With respect
As a matter of fact
As far as I am concerned
I am of the opinion that

# SENTENCE LENGTH

Short sentences are easier to read than long sentences, though a text made up entirely of short sentences sounds stilted and reads badly. To make the text interesting, a variety of sentence lengths and structures are needed. First of all you'll consider writing short sentences and then you'll meet 'signpost' words to help you create sentences that flow together well.

Long sentences with many clauses can be difficult to understand – remember your writing is competing with lots of other information. If it's hard to read, people will put it aside and may never get round to looking at it.

With highly specialist content, there may be unfamiliar or difficult words and concepts. When the content is complicated, aim for around 15-20 words per sentence because your message is easier to understand when sentences are shorter.

# SENTENCE LENGTH

Compare these two paragraphs and decide which is easier to understand:

> The reason long sentences are hard to read is that your short-term memory gets overloaded before you reach the end of the sentence and you forget what was said at the start and have to go back and re-read earlier parts of the sentence, or start putting in additional punctuation such as commas to try to make it easier to understand. **(61 words)**

> Long sentences are harder to read because your short-term memory is overloaded before you reach the end of the sentence. You forget what was said at the start and have to go back and re-read earlier parts of the sentence. Writers may add additional punctuation such as commas to try to make it easier to understand. **(Total word count per sentence: 21 + 20 + 16)**

Most people find the second paragraph easier to take in.

# SIGNPOST WORDS

As children you learned to write in short sentences. Eg, *The cat sat on the mat. The cat is black. The cat drinks milk.*

This sounds disjointed, and the text doesn't flow. As your writing skills developed, you learned to connect related ideas into longer sentences with linking words. Some of these refer to something earlier in the text and others signpost forward.

Imagine yourself driving down a familiar country road. If there were no road signs you would still be able to drive safely, because you know the road. But on an unfamiliar road the signs warn you about the road ahead. Without them you would have to proceed cautiously.

Similarly, signpost words signal what is coming next and help your readers to interpret the meaning of the text.

# SIGNPOST WORDS

Contrast the next two texts without and with linking words. Which do you think best conveys its message?

Standing on an expensive, crowded, commuter train seems unfair and bad value. There are few options. Crawling along congested roads in a car is even worse. We are seeing a change in working patterns. Technology and changing attitudes enable many people to work remotely. We don't need to travel every day. We can work from home, have phone meetings and communicate, via email. People need contact with their colleagues. Face-to-face meetings help to build relationships. They provide the social contact – an important motivator for many people at work.

# SIGNPOST WORDS

Standing on an expensive, crowded, commuter train seems unfair and bad value, **but** there are few options **as** crawling along congested roads in a car is even worse. However, we are seeing a change in working patterns, **as** technology and changing attitudes enable many people to work remotely. We don't need to travel every day **since** we can work from home, have phone meetings and communicate via email. **Nevertheless**, people need contact with their colleagues, **so** face-to-face meetings help to build relationships **and** provide the social contact **that is** an important motivator for many people at work.

The linking words in the second text help the reader to interpret and understand the text and it flows better. Do you agree?

# SIGNPOST WORDS

Here are the signpost words used in the previous paragraph along with other frequently used linking words:

- And
- But
- As
- However
- Since
- Nevertheless
- So
- That

- Therefore
- Hence
- Although
- Which
- Thus
- Then
- Firstly
- Also

- As well as
- Besides
- Furthermore
- In addition
- Plus
- Moreover
- But
- Despite

- Formerly
- Previously
- Because
- Consequently
- Finally

Which ones do you use regularly? Are there any you have never used?

You need a balance between keeping sentences short and using linking words to connect ideas and to make the writing flow.

# PUT THE MAIN POINT FIRST IN SENTENCES

**Put Key Information First** is a good rule for sentences as well as for the structure of your writing. Put important information early in the sentence, so the reader knows immediately what you are talking about.

Put Key Information **1st**

EXAMPLE

*'Having been established and growing for at least twenty five years, the beech tree is now shading the neighbours' patio and they have requested that it is pruned.'*

The reader has to wait for the second clause before the key point and their short-term memory is loaded with information before they get there.

EXAMPLE

This sentence could be written:

*'The neighbours have asked for the beech tree to be pruned as it is shading their patio. The tree is at least twenty five years old.'*

The brain recognises the topic of the sentence and can start to interpret it quickly.

(49)

# ACTIVE VERSUS PASSIVE VOICE

You may have heard people talk about writing in the active or passive voice. You will find it explained here and understand why using an active construction makes your writing simpler and more concise.

The simplest form of a sentence is to put the 'Agent' at the beginning – active construction.

| Agent: the thing doing the action | Verb: the action word | The Target: the thing being acted on |
|---|---|---|
| The boy | kicked | the ball. |
| The computer system | checks | the credit ratings. |

# ACTIVE VERSUS PASSIVE VOICE

Writers can change the emphasis by reversing the sentence structure so that you get a passive construction.

| The Target:<br>the thing being acted on | Verb:<br>the action word | Agent:<br>person or thing doing the action |
| --- | --- | --- |
| The ball | was kicked | by the boy. |
| The credit ratings | are checked | by the computer system. |

This is perfectly acceptable if you have a good reason for choosing the passive voice, ie if the ball is what you're interested in. However, the passive construction makes the sentence longer and more complicated.

Readers find documents more engaging and easier to understand when you write in the active voice.

# AVOID NOMINALISATIONS

A nominalisation (verbal noun) is a noun made out of a verb. Examples: adjust – verb, adjustment – noun

**Active:** The operator **adjusts** the temperature.
**Passive:** The temperature is **adjusted** by the operator.
**Nominalisation:** An **adjustment** is made to the temperature by the operator.

The sentence gets progressively longer because you need to add a verb back into the sentence. To identify nominalisations look out for common verbs like 'carried out', 'made', 'undertaken' and words ending in '-ment', '-tion' and '-ing.' This usually indicates the main verb has been nominalised.

People use more nominalisations and passive verbs when they are lacking in confidence and are trying to impress a reader or distance themselves from the message. Research consistently shows people are impressed by simpler language and believe the writers are more intelligent, clearer thinkers and even nicer people!

# COMMUNICATE PERSONALLY RATHER THAN IMPERSONALLY

When you're talking you use people's names and talk about *you, he, she* – by referring directly to people you create a personal tone, even in a formal setting. This builds relationships and also makes it clear who is responsible or needs to take action.

Sometimes when you're writing you may find you've slipped into an impersonal mode, believing it is more formal and 'the correct thing to do'. Avoiding personal references can lead to complexity or ambiguity, so consider carefully what you want to say, rather than use the impersonal as a default structure.

For example you might write: *'Safety checks on fire extinguishers must be carried out properly'*. Who will actually carry out these checks? It would be quite easy for everyone to agree with the statement but nobody to do the safety checks. *'The safety officer must carry out the proper safety checks on the fire extinguishers'* is a clearer alternative.

Think about your purpose before slipping into the impersonal mode – your writing will be read by a real person and not a faceless mass.

# PARAGRAPHS

Now you've thought about words and sentences you need to consider paragraphs. A page of text with no paragraphs is off-putting and hard to read. By breaking your text into paragraphs you make it easier to read and digest and you guide your reader through your document.

The rule that you  **Put Key Information 1st** applies to paragraphs as well as to sentences and to your whole document structure.

Rules for paragraphs:
- One idea per paragraph
- Start each paragraph with a sentence to introduce the main idea
- Expand on this in the rest of the paragraph

You should be able to understand the main elements of a document by just reading the first sentence in every paragraph. This is a technique taught in speed reading – if you bury your main idea in the middle of a paragraph then it may not get read.

# PHASE 2: WRITING CLEARLY & CONCISELY

# PUNCTUATION IN BRIEF

We've answered the most commonly asked questions here. For more information or for regular reference we suggest you buy a book on punctuation and check it when in doubt. Our rule is to keep it as simple as possible.

**Full Stops**
Capital letters start sentences; full stops end them.

**Commas**
Use commas

- Where you need to pause,

- To separate clauses in a sentence: *'The house, which is in need of complete renovation, is for sale.'*

- Between items in a list: *'Buckets, spades, suncream, hats and raincoats are all useful at the beach.'*

# PUNCTUATION IN BRIEF

**Semi colons** have three purposes:

1. Between two strongly linked independent sentences, for example:
   *The conference is in Manchester; there will be one thousand delegates.*

2. To show contrast: *I love writing; John hates it.*

3. In lists where the items are lengthy: *Multiple choice exams; written essay questions; online test-yourself quizzes.*

**Colons** can be used:

1. To introduce bulleted and numbered lists (as above) and horizontal lists, eg *We are missing the following: dots, stripes and crosses.*

2. To introduce direct speech and quotations, eg *John hissed: 'It's the punctuation section!'*

3. When the second half of a sentence expands, explains or summarises the first half, eg *The car is unreliable: it is hard to start.*

# PUNCTUATION IN BRIEF

**Apostrophes show possession:**
Maurice's book = the book belonging to Maurice.
When there are plurals, the apostrophe goes after the s: *'The writers' pencils were blunt'*
(many writers), versus: *'The writer's pencils were blunt'* (a single writer).

**Apostrophes also show a letter is missing** – usually when a letter is removed to
shorten a word: *'Don't get off the bus'* instead of *'Do not get off the bus.'*

Which brings us to **it's** and **its**...
**It's** is the shortened form of it is: *It's my favourite book.*

**Its** doesn't have an apostrophe because it's a possessive pronoun like *yours, his, hers,
ours;* none of which has an apostrophe.

Here's the difference: **It's** my dog and **its** wooden leg is loose.

# LAYOUT: MAKE YOUR DOCUMENT STAND OUT

Latin writing didn't have spaces between words – theyjoinedallthewordsup. It made reading much harder but papyrus was in short supply and people had more time to read.

Your documents are competing with many other distractions for a reader's attention. Layout can make the difference between someone picking up your document or putting it on the 'to do later' pile – where it may never be read!

Documents need to be visually and mentally accessible to as many readers as possible. Guide your reader's eyes around your document so they can find the information they want quickly and easily as they scan it.

Organisations sometimes have rules about layout to make documents look tidy but they may not make reading simpler. Use the information following to challenge standards.

# LAYOUT: MAKE YOUR DOCUMENT STAND OUT

Information from the British Dyslexia Association and RNIB suggests documents are easier to read when you use:

- 12 point font as the minimum
- Sans serif fonts such as Arial, Comic Sans, Verdana
- Capitals in the appropriate place which lead readers' eyes around the page
- About 60 to 70 characters per line
- Paragraphs, and lines between them, to break up blocks of dense text
- Left justified lines with a ragged right edge (like this)
- Two spaces between sentences
- Space of 1.5 or 2 between lines
- **Bold typeface** to highlight rather than *italics* or <u>underlining</u>
- A contrast between text and background – contrast is also affected by size and weight of the font

# LAYOUT: MAKE YOUR DOCUMENT STAND OUT

*Fancy or complicated fonts are not so easy to read — this font had to be increased to 15 points to make it readable.*

Changing fonts ***all the time*** can be very irritating. Fonts with little space between the letters are also hard to read.

Lines that are too long
or too short can put strain on
the eyes

Lines that are right justified are harder to read.

Justification and columns with the same margin at either end of the page makes the lines look neat at either end, but can make words appear to swim around as the spaces vary — the white space can be more distracting than the words, particularly for readers with dyslexia.

# ILLUSTRATIONS: WHY PICTURES TELL A THOUSAND WORDS

People evolved to process visual information long before anyone invented writing, so you're naturally very good at interpreting pictures. Consider all the pictures or symbols you see every day: traffic signs, washing instructions, symbols on machinery, company logos, etc; they are universal. To use words instead would occupy more space and take longer both to write and to read.

Illustrations, pictures or graphics are generally used to:

- Strengthen a point in an explanation or argument
- Make data available as reference
- Make information accessible to more people
- Add interest and increase concentration
- Offer a range of reading strategies

See http://www.visual-literacy.org/periodic_table/periodic_table.html for creative ideas on displaying information visually.

# PICTURES, DIAGRAMS & PHOTOGRAPHS

Keep illustrations simple and clear and consider all the implications your picture may generate – a picture is worth a thousand words. If you plan to re-use an illustration in another document check that it's still appropriate. Consider, also, whether colour images will still be visible if copied in black and white.

- Label illustrations so readers don't have to keep cross-referencing to the text
- Provide an explanatory title
- Put the illustration on the same page as explanatory text
- Use simple bold diagrams with clean lines
- Ensure resolution of photographs is high enough to be clear
- Size, format and crop pictures to select relevant parts
- Adjust the contrast for optimum clarity
- Compress photos before inserting into text
- Check and respect copyright

# TOP TIPS FOR TABLES

Many of the rules for tables are the same as for diagrams and pictures. Additionally:

- Use explanatory headers written in bold
- Think about how you will divide up columns and rows
- Fully lined tables may look too busy
- White space can be used to divide rows and columns
- Decide on horizontal or vertical lines depending on how you want to lead the reader's eye around the page
- Elements to be compared are usually listed vertically while variables are listed horizontally
- Readers expect to move from known material on the left to new information on the right
- Use bold text or colour as highlights
- In technical reports use a symbol to indicate an absence of data, rather than 0
- Put large amounts of raw data in appendices

# ILLUSTRATIONS: GUIDANCE FOR GRAPHS

Different graphs have different purposes; pie charts are helpful for information about time or proportion; bar charts compare data. Follow the same general guidelines for illustrations.

Mention the graph in the text, before you present it on the page.

People read down the page, so we suggest putting an informative title above the graph.

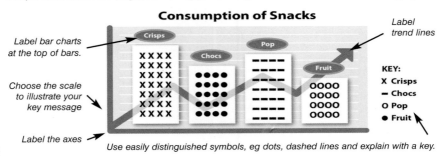

**Consumption of Snacks**

*Label bar charts at the top of bars.*

*Choose the scale to illustrate your key message*

*Label the axes*

*Label trend lines*

KEY:
X Crisps
− Chocs
O Pop
● Fruit

*Use easily distinguished symbols, eg dots, dashed lines and explain with a key.*

# HOW TO WRITE A SUMMARY

Longer documents may need an informative summary to provide key messages in a concise format. Before starting to write your summary you need to think about your purpose and your readers (you may have heard us mention this before.)

Look at the next sales leaflet you see. There will be an attention grabbing statement at the top summarising the product and what it can do for you. Its purpose is to hook your attention and to get you to read further.

In a CV, a profile statement gives a punchy four line summary of the candidate – what they are and their key attributes. The purpose of the profile statement is to make a first positive impression, to get the recruiter's attention and to make it into the short-listing pile.

Try writing a tweet to summarise your document – only 140 characters allowed!

# HOW TO WRITE A SUMMARY

The purpose of a summary is usually for a busy reader to see the conclusions or recommendations and decide whether to read on. It is also an opportunity to read the key facts twice and to prepare for the main text.

Write the summary last but position it first.

● Use your original plan to help you identify key points
● Read through the document and highlight the key points and information
● Make a mind-map of key information
● Number the key points in order of importance to the reader

Now write the summary from these notes. The order of information in a summary will not necessarily be the same as in the main document.

**A summary is not a forum for new information.** Only include ideas which are already explored in the main document.

# SUMMARY STYLE & STRUCTURE

## AN INFORMATIVE SUMMARY

Present the information in the order of greatest importance to the readers. Hence summaries with different purposes have different structures.

### Recommendations for action:
- Recommended action first
- Main reasons for the recommendation
- Cost, savings, timings and a short version of key evidence

### Reports for knowledge capture or for the record:
- One or two sentences to summarise the introduction, background and objectives
- A few sentences to summarise the work and quantified results
- State the main conclusions and recommendations

# SUMMARY STYLE & STRUCTURE

## A SALES SUMMARY

With a sale summary the purpose is to hook the reader and get them to buy. It needs to:
- Be punchy and impactful
- Say what the product is
- Describe its unique benefits
- Set out what it can do for the prospective buyer

So Stella and I might write a sales summary about ourselves: *'Innovative management development consultants working with FTSE 100 companies and SMEs, Beth and Stella can help your organisation succeed through excellent communication!'*

Or for a robotic floor-cleaner:

*'Let Dobbie, the robotic floor-cleaner, take the hard work out of cleaning the floors. Ideal for wood, stone and tile floors, simply set Dobbie going while you put your feet up!'*

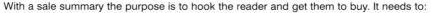

**PHASE 3**

**Reviewing & Polishing**
- Forget It
- Being concise
- Critiquing and proofreading

## PHASE 3: REVIEWING & POLISHING

# FORGET IT

Few people get their first draft entirely right, so in Phase 3 of our writing process you will learn to critique and proofread your writing. Before you do so, however, there is an important first step – put your work (even a short note or email) on one side and forget it!

The importance of accuracy in writing is vital to create a good impression. When you speak people often overlook errors because you can move on quickly, or correct them, but people can return to a document many times and the errors are always there.

When you have been immersed in the writing it's much harder to spot mistakes or to review it effectively because your brain sees what it expects to see. Depending on the size of the work, or its importance to you, set it aside for:
- A few days
- Overnight
- A few hours
- A short time to have a break and do something else

You will then return invigorated, able to review your writing with fresh eyes and brain.

# HOW CONCISE IS YOUR WRITING?

One of the most frequent questions we are asked is *'How can I be more concise?'* Use this checklist as the first part of your reviewing activity.

1. Be precise – use numbers, measurements or statistics for clarity
2. Ruthlessly eliminate redundant words
3. Avoid unnecessary description – do you need the adjectives (eg the **fluffy** rabbit) and adverbs (eg swimming **swiftly**)
4. Leave out weak words – *quite, very, pretty* (as in 'a pretty long road'), *almost, fairly, quickly, slowly, nicely, timely, kind of, sort of*
5. Use active rather than passive constructions (see pages 50-51)
6. Avoid nominalisations (see page 52)
7. Consider deleting *'that'* – it occurs frequently but can often be removed without altering your meaning

PHASE 3: REVIEWING & POLISHING

# HOW CONCISE IS YOUR WRITING?

This is another useful exercise to practise occasionally. You'll find lots of possibilities for 'pruning'.

```
┌──────────────┐        ┌──────────────┐        ┌──────────────┐
│ Write your   │        │ Edit the     │        │ Can you cut  │
│ document     │        │ document to  │        │ it further   │
│ as well as   │        │ cut your     │        │ and still    │
│ you can      │        │ word count   │        │ make sense   │
│              │        │ by an        │        │ of it?       │
│              │        │ arbitrary 25%│        │              │
└──────────────┘        └──────────────┘        └──────────────┘

     ┌──────────────┐        ┌──────────────┐        ┌──────────────┐
     │ Do a word    │        │ Read it      │        │ Make a note  │
     │ count        │        │ through      │        │ of your      │
     │ (your        │        │ again to     │        │ habits to    │
     │ software     │        │ ensure it    │        │ watch out    │
     │ should do    │        │ makes sense  │        │ for later    │
     │ this for you)│        │              │        │              │
     └──────────────┘        └──────────────┘        └──────────────┘
```

72

# CRITIQUING & PROOFREADING

When you're critiquing and reviewing you need to ask yourself questions like:
- Does the writing flow?
- Is there a logical structure?
- Will the reader be able to find the information they need easily?

What are you looking for when you proofread?
- Spelling errors and typing mistakes
- Punctuation and grammar
- Consistency of layout

We suggest you separate the task into doing your own critiquing first and then proofreading. If it's a large or particularly important piece of work, enlist the help of a colleague to critique first before you proofread, and then ask someone else to proofread as well.

# REVIEWING & CRITIQUING

On pages 75-77 we have provided a critiquing checklist which you can use to:

- Review your own document
- Give to a colleague and ask them to review your document

When you're critiquing you're making sure that what you've written will make sense to your reader – they only have your words to rely on. They can't see your gestures or your body language, they can't hear your voice and they can't read your mind. You have to help them interpret everything you want to communicate using only words.

# PHASE 3: REVIEWING & POLISHING

## CRITIQUING CHECKLIST

Go through the document and ask the following questions:

### Purpose
- What is the purpose of your document and what do you want to achieve?

### Reader
- Who will your readers be?
- What is their knowledge of the subject and what information do they need?
- What do you want them to do as a result of this communication?

### Medium
- Have you chosen an appropriate medium? (Eg, letter, email, notice, web page, etc)

### Structure
- Is the structure of the document obvious and well signposted?
- Is the structure appropriate?

# CRITIQUING CHECKLIST

**Can the reader find the information they need?**
- Is the title consistent with the scope of the document?
- Is there a summary if necessary and does it cover the main points?
- Are headings and numbering systems clear and explanatory? Will they help the reader navigate around the document?
- Is the key information obvious to the reader?

**Paragraphs and layout**
- Have paragraphs been used to divide the text into readable chunks?
- Does the first sentence tell the reader the topic of the paragraph?
- Are the chunks arranged in a logical order?
- Is the layout visually attractive with plenty of white space?

**Sentences**
- Are sentences fairly short (15 to 20 words), but still vary in length?
- Are sentences clear and simple with the main point at the start?
- Is the text written in the active or passive voice?

## PHASE 3: REVIEWING & POLISHING

# CRITIQUING CHECKLIST

### Choice of words
- Are the ideas expressed using simple, clear words?
- Are there any redundant and unnecessary words?
- Will the readers understand any technical terms or jargon?

### Content
- Is the content suitable for the purpose and the reader?
- Is there any unnecessary information, ambiguity or repetition?
- Is there enough data to justify the conclusions and recommendations?
- Is the level of detail suitable for the purpose?

### Illustrations, tables and charts
- Are illustrations, tables, diagrams and graphs well set out and labelled and appropriately cross-referenced to the text?

**Does the document achieve its objectives?**

# TEN TOP TIPS FOR PROOFREADING

When you are familiar with the content of your document, it is hard to spot errors. Techniques for proofreading slow you down to see what is actually written on the page; rather than what you think is there.

1. Use your software to do a spelling and grammar check – they are not totally reliable, so follow up with other types of proofreading.
2. Print out your document to make it easier to find mistakes.
3. Read it out loud to a partner and look and listen for errors.
4. Use your senses when proofreading – look at it, sound it out, run your finger along word by word.
5. Go down the page with a ruler reading only one line at a time.
6. Check all proper names and special terminology.
7. Read backwards, word by word; a good way to spot typos or spelling mistakes.
8. Read backwards sentence by sentence for unclear sentence structures.
9. Check consistency of layout, eg fonts, bold, headings.
10. Look for consistent error patterns – words you commonly misspell or incorrect sentence constructions – and keep a checklist.

**Getting the Tone Right**
- Getting the reaction you want
- Building rapport
- Writing clearly and assertively
- Ideas for influencing your reader

GETTING THE TONE RIGHT

# TAKE PEOPLE WITH YOU

Our three phase process for writing has shown you how to take a structured and speedy approach to producing a written communication that will achieve its objectives.

So far we haven't specifically covered the tone of your writing and how people will feel when they read it. We are treating this as a separate chapter to give it the importance it deserves – you need to consider the tone of your writing at an early stage when writing your drafts. It is really an expansion of the question 'who is my reader?' and part of choosing your words carefully.

This chapter will help you to get the tone of your writing right, so you can get your point over clearly and get the action you want, while still considering the emotional needs of your reader. This part of the book will help you to communicate effectively and 'take people with you'.

# REDUCED LEVEL OF COMMUNICATION

When you speak to people face to face you can see their response by observing their body language and hearing their voice. You get immediate feedback about the other person's reactions and can compose the next part of your message accordingly.

On the phone, you lose the visual channel, but can still hear how the person responds and adjust your message to suit the conversation.

In writing, you lose both the visual and auditory channels of communication and rely on your words alone. This makes it very important to choose the words carefully to get the response you want.

In this chapter, you will explore ways of conveying your meaning clearly and assertively while building good relationships through written communication. The advice we give will apply to all types of writing eg letters, sales literature, blogs and web-pages, but email is often the one where you have most opportunity to build relationships.

# WHY YOU DON'T ALWAYS GET THE REACTION YOU WANT

Have you ever sent an email and then been surprised by the response – perhaps it seemed uncooperative or they didn't do what you asked? It could be that the person was in a bad mood or too busy, but perhaps, unwittingly, you wrote something that irritated the other person, or you wrote non-assertively.

In general it is wise to express yourself in writing moderately but unmistakably. You may get away with being heated in conversation, but when you write, your message may come across bluntly and stimulate a strong response. Or, if you express yourself too timidly, you may not get your point across to the reader.

So, on the next pages you will find some simple ways to express yourself directly, constructively and assertively. Our definition of assertiveness is that you take account of your own needs and rights and also those of the other person. So assertiveness is a balanced and reasonable behaviour, working towards a mutually constructive outcome.

# CREATING RAPPORT IN WRITING

Rapport is an invisible thread connecting two people which gives them a sense of ease and a good relationship. When you meet people face to face you start to build rapport by smiling, shaking hands and greeting them warmly. You may ask them about their journey, or their weekend or their family.

Through these simple social interactions you build up an area of common interest and get the communication flowing in a relaxed manner. You are building and cementing the relationship before you get on with the business of the day.

You can also build rapport in writing with a friendly greeting and a sentence or two of social chat. Contrast the difference in tone between an email with only a straight request or instruction and one which starts off with some rapport building.

# CREATING RAPPORT IN WRITING

Contrast two emails; first a straightforward, but slightly blunt one:

> Asif,
> I want you to do a presentation to the team next week, so can you get your slides to me by this afternoon for approval. **Fred**

See how the tone changes with this one where we have worked to build rapport.

> Hello Asif,
> I hope you had a good holiday and your daughter is settling in well at school. I am away at a conference next week so I would like you to make a presentation to the team. Please will you get your slides to me by this afternoon for approval? **Thanks Fred**

You can see that small changes build rapport and change the tone.

# BE CLEAR & ASSERTIVE

You can build your writing with three types of assertive sentences, mixing and matching them as required: basic statements, open questions, and conveying empathy. These are covered in the next few pages.

### 1. Basic Statements
- To give information
- State our views
- State our needs or beliefs

Use 'I' statements rather than 'it', 'you', and 'one'. 'I' statements are direct, powerful and assertive. It is clear that you are giving your own opinion.
- I can, I think
- I believe, I feel
- I like
- I'd like you to
- I prefer
- I will
- I won't be able to .....

# BE CLEAR & ASSERTIVE

### 2. Open questions
Open questions are one of your most valuable communication tools to find out information or ask about someone else's views, opinions or needs or position. They usually start with *Who, Why, Where, What, When and How* and require more than a 'yes' or 'no' answer. They are very useful when you want to reach a win-win solution.

**Examples of open questions:**

What do you think?

When could you do this?

Who would be the best person for this?

How do you feel about this?

Why would that be a concern?

Where would you like to meet?

# BE CLEAR & ASSERTIVE

### 3. Conveying empathy

Displaying empathy is acknowledging another person's position or feelings; it's when you put yourself in the other person's shoes and show you can see things from their perspective as well as your own. You use empathy to build a bridge between yourself and other people.

### Examples:
- I recognise....
- I understand....
- I appreciate....
- I realise.....and....

Be careful using the word 'but' when conveying empathy. It can be seen to diminish everything that has gone before: *'I hear you but...'.* You can build on what you've said by using 'and' – *'I hear you and...'.* ('However' and 'yet' are like a polite 'but'.)

## GETTING THE TONE RIGHT

# BE CLEAR & ASSERTIVE

Occasionally you may need to be stronger in your written dealings with other people. This can seem more difficult, particularly if it is something you feel will upset them such as:

- Pointing out when someone has not done what they agreed to do
- Conveying your own negative feelings about a situation in a controlled and constructive way
- Issuing an ultimatum and giving someone a last chance to take action

Here are some techniques to deal with these types of situations.

GETTING THE TONE RIGHT

# POINTING OUT A DISCREPANCY

If you want to remind someone of something they have agreed to, but not yet done, try using a sentence like this.

EXAMPLE

> 'On August 26th we agreed that you would provide the information for my project. I haven't received the data yet, and this means that we will be really pushed to meet the deadline. So please will you update me on where you have got to by tomorrow morning.'

The structure here is:
- State what was agreed
- State that it hasn't happened yet
- Get information in order to plan the way forward

*Acknowledgements to Ken and Kate Back for their classification of assertive language.*

# EXPRESSING YOUR FEELINGS

When you feel worked up, it is easy to let your emotion spill onto the page. Sometimes you want people to know how you feel about a situation or their behaviour so you need a format to express your feelings in a controlled, clear and constructive way.

A useful structure for this type of situation is:

SITUATION  BEHAVIOUR  IMPACT  ACTION

# GETTING THE TONE RIGHT

## EXPRESSING YOUR FEELINGS

An email written using Situation, Behaviour, Impact, Action.

| Bcc: | |
|------|---|
| Subject: | Signature: Signature #1 |
| From: | john <john@efire-design.com> |

How did you think the meeting with Mrs Smith went this morning? While we came out with an action plan, I left feeling uncomfortable and now want to share my concerns with you. Several times in the meeting, I felt you were rude and offhand with me in front of the client. You actually told me to 'shut up!' at one point. I feel this is unprofessional and gives the department a bad reputation.

Clearly we need to work together with Mrs Smith, so would you like to go for a coffee and we can discuss how we work together more constructively in the future?

GETTING THE TONE RIGHT

# GIVING AN ULTIMATUM – A LAST CHANCE TO ACT

When you have tried every other option, you may need to issue an ultimatum or a sanction. Think carefully about it as you lose power if you do not carry it out.

I remember saying to my daughter when she was young, *'If you don't behave you will not be able to go to the party.'* I was taken aback when she said, *'Good, I didn't want to go anyway!'* I regretted my words as I saw my peaceful afternoon disappearing and I will leave you to guess what happened next!

With a sanction or ultimatum, you need to firmly explain the consequences.

EXAMPLE

*'I need your timesheet by 9am on the 20th of each month. If you do not supply it, unfortunately you will not be paid that month. Please make sure you get it in promptly.'*

# WORDS TO BE WARY OF

**Uncertainties**
- Perhaps/ maybe
- Hopefully
- Try

**Using rules against yourself**
- I ought
- I should

**Over apologising**
- I'm terribly sorry

**Asking others**
- Do you think I ought to

**Put downs**
- It's just a ...

**Hopelessness**
- We can't do anything
- It's hopeless

**Imposing rules on others**
- You must
- You should

**Generalisations**
- Everyone always
- It's never...

**Expressing opinion as facts**
- It's like this

**Making decisions for others**
- If I were you

**Blaming others**
- If you hadn't done that
- Why on earth did you do that?

**Giving orders**
- Get me that data now

## GETTING THE TONE RIGHT

# IDEAS FOR INFLUENCING YOUR READER

One of the key purposes for writing is to influence or persuade people. You can apply some of the same influencing tactics in writing as you use face to face.

- Know your objective
- Find out as much as you can about the readers
- WIIFT – What's in it for them? Benefits? Reduction of pain?
- Why might they object?
- Reduce resistance and opposition and make it easy for them to accept
- Use constructive and outcome focused language (see following pages)
- Use 'I' statements
- Active voice is more persuasive than passive
- Personal voice is more persuasive than impersonal
- Structure your case
- Build rapport and a relationship – people are influenced by people they like
- Display your expertise and authority
- Choose the best medium – a formal letter, an informal email, a text message?

# INFLUENCING: OUTCOME FOCUSED LANGUAGE

To increase your influence, be more credible and reduce conflict, express yourself constructively. How often do you tell people what you don't want to happen? For example, *'That's not how I want it!'; 'Don't drive so fast!'*.

You can't process a negative thought without first processing the direct words you see or hear. Try not thinking about a Ferrari.

When you read 'Don't drive so fast' your brain subconsciously connects first to memories and knowledge about fast driving. Those thoughts need to be suppressed before you can think about slow driving and that process uses more energy. To avoid making your readers work hard you need to make it easy for them to understand, so tell them what you want, rather than what you don't want.

If you don't tell people specifically what you want, they have to infer it and may still get it wrong; driving at 50mph instead of 70mph, when what you wanted was a sedate 30mph.

# INFLUENCING: OUTCOME FOCUSED LANGUAGE

Compare these sentences: identify what has been changed and consider why.

**Negative Focus:** Don't forget to send that message to the boss.

**Outcome Focus:** Remember to send that message to the boss.

**Negative Focus:** Never turn off the computer without backing-up.

**Outcome Focus:** Always back-up the computer before you turn it off.

**Negative Focus:** Please don't hesitate to contact me if there's anything you can't understand.

**Outcome Focus:** Please phone me if you have any questions.

Outcome focused constructive language leads to a positive expectation, a clearer visualisation of the goal and you are more likely to get your desired result.

**HITs: Hints, Ideas & Tips**
- Writing on screen
- Email etiquette
- Signing on and off
- Some common errors to avoid
- Writing in a global business world

# INTRODUCTION

This final section of the book covers a range of hints, ideas and tips that people tell us they have found useful. They cover:

- Writing on screen rather than paper
- Electronic media
- Email etiquette
- Signing on and signing off
- Writing in a global world
- Some common errors to avoid

# WRITING FOR SCREENS

Nowadays most of what you write appears on screens rather than paper. There is plenty of research and debate as to what makes for a good 'on-screen' reading experience and whether you need to adjust your writing styles, layouts, fonts to compensate. As people become more used to reading from screens they seem to be adapting their reading methods.

Some of what you write will only be relevant and read for a short time but it's almost always stored on a server somewhere. You can't just screw up the paper, burn it and it's gone.

So be aware of what you're writing, who'll read it and what the long term impact may be. Tweets, emails, blogs etc can be used as legal evidence and some business communication systems have audit trails so electronic writing and all alterations are tracked.

Electronic information also has metadata; for example the date and time a document was written could be useful in a copyright case.

# WRITING FOR SCREENS

Reading on electronic media is different from reading from paper. Generally people read 25% slower on a computer screen compared to a printed page and it's less accurate, more fatiguing, decreases comprehension and is rated inferior by readers themselves. They may be engaged in a shallower, less focused way than with printed text so you need to take this into account.

If you're writing for the web, users are impatient and critical – we all suffer from information overload and people usually expect one 'page down' or 'scroll down' action per document.

Readers tend to scan the page instead of reading word by word so slow down their scanning with bulleted and numbered lists. While graphics add value you need to be aware they take longer to download than text.

# WRITING FOR THE SCREEN: GENERAL TIPS

When you're writing for a screen:
- Use bullets and numbered lists to draw attention to important points
- Use half the word count for a web page to its paper equivalent
- Make online documents concise and scannable
- Highlight key words
- Avoid italicizing as it slows down online reading
- Use links to encourage people to explore your information

Many of your readers will still print your documents to read them. While it is easier for you to write many pages without using up paper, your readers may be using whole trees in printing off your documents.

Did you know 40 gigabytes of data could amount to 20 metric tonnes of printed paper?

# ELECTRONIC MEDIA

It's simple to write texts, instant messages, tweets, etc, quickly press 'send' and then sometimes regret it. They are even more reduced forms of communication than normal writing, which is why they can easily be misunderstood.

The advantage of writing over face-to-face communication is you have time to plan it, even if only for a few moments.

With electronic communications think:
- What's my outcome – what do I want the person to do?
- How will they feel about this message? How do I want them to feel?
- What's the best way to transmit this message? Is it data or emotions I'm sending?
- What's the context; will it make sense to someone else?

Most importantly, step into your reader's shoes and read your message before you press 'send'. You've still got time to edit it!

# EMAIL ETIQUETTE

Email is both a faster way to deliver information and a communication tool itself.

Before you write, decide whether you really need to pass on the information and who needs to know? Have you checked whether email is the best way to communicate? If the email is longer than half a screen put the information in an attachment.

Remember every email creates work for someone:
- Use the 'To' box for those who need to take action
- Use 'CC' only for those who really need to know (CC means Carbon Copy)
- Use 'Reply To All' sparingly
- Avoid long address lists
- Avoid 'BCC' unless sending to multiple users who don't want to share email addresses (BCC stands for Blind Carbon Copy)

# EMAIL ETIQUETTE

Composing your message:

- Use an informative title
- Keep to a single subject to aid recognition, filing and retrieval
- Build rapport with a friendly greeting
- Put the most important information in the first paragraph
- Format well for easy reading
- Use correct grammar to ensure clarity and accuracy and to avoid ambiguity
- Choose your words carefully
- Don't be a novelist – emails are concise and to the point
- Send links as an alternative to large attachments
- Use 'high priority' and 'read receipts' only when needed
- Put your contact details at the bottom of emails

Take care – emails are easily forwarded on, inside or outside the organisation.

# MANAGING EMOTION IN EMAILS

Emails can be misinterpreted because they are less formal and are read in the mood of the receiver rather than the mood of the sender. And it's very easy to respond quickly without thinking – so remember to plan and check before pressing 'send'.

- Be careful with humour; comments may be interpreted differently without visual cues
- Don't respond in anger (or any strong emotion). Wait for it to subside, re-read the message and write a considered response. Or phone and discuss the issue
- Choose your words carefully; *'I'm angry'* may raise a reader's defences, whereas *'surprised', 'frustrated', 'disappointed'* will get your message across more accurately
- If it's sensitive ask someone else to review your message before you send it
- Be diplomatic – comments seem harsher when written
- Don't carry out sensitive management tasks via email
- A short email to say thank you will always be appreciated

# SIGNING ON & SIGNING OFF

Because of the wide use of email people often write more informally now than in the past but it's still useful to know how to start and sign off emails and letters.

Use the principles of building rapport to help you build relationships in your writing. If someone has written to you first you can use their greeting as an indication of how they would like to be addressed – mirror their use of language where appropriate.

If you are the first to write it's advisable to be slightly more formal than less formal. Starting a first email to someone you don't know with 'Dear Jane' or even 'Dear Miss Jones' is better than 'Hi Jane' but if they respond with 'Hi Jack' then it's appropriate to shift to their greeting.

People like to have their names used, so even if someone starts an email to you without your name, use their name in your response because it builds relationships.

# SIGNING ON & SIGNING OFF

- Letters are usually more formal than emails, even when email is used as a delivery tool for a letter
- 'Dear Sir' is signed off as 'Yours faithfully'
- 'Dear Mrs Patel' is signed off as 'Yours sincerely'
- The most common sign off for business emails is 'Regards' but there are no hard and fast rules
- Using an automatic signature on emails helps readers because they know who you are, your role and how else they can contact you – it's all about making communication easier
- Make it easy – set up automatic signatures in your email system so you don't have to write them out each time. As a minimum, give your name, position and telephone number but you may also include your postal address, your skype name, website, Linked In details or twitter name

# WRITING IN A GLOBAL BUSINESS WORLD

In this global business world you may find you write to people in other cultures, time zones, environments and who speak different languages. Writing directly and simply becomes even more important and you need to be aware of cultural gaffes (see Cross-Cultural Business Pocketbook).

Easy things to avoid or look out for:

- Avoid slang or colloquialisms specific to your culture or language eg *'the project has gone off the boil'*
- Use clear assertive language
- Avoid waffle: 'it may or may not be...'
- Be consistent in spellings: *'...ise'* or *'...ize'* endings
- Be tolerant of people doing things differently from you
- Keep sentences short and use simple construction
- Use pictures or diagrams to explain difficult concepts where you can
- Keep a list of words or phrases that mean something different in other projects, companies, countries or cultures

Remember what's normal for you is different to someone else!

# SOME COMMON IRRITATIONS TO AVOID

People have very different tolerance levels to written communication and little things can distract them from your point. Here are some commonly expressed irritations to avoid.

- Split infinitives eg 'To boldly go' – we're very familiar with this one but whenever you split 'to' from the 'verb' it's a split infinitive. It's not wrong but can distract some readers. If possible find another way to say the same thing

- Yourself, myself – instead of 'you' or 'me'. Sometimes people think this makes their writing seem more businesslike but it's usually incorrect. Eg 'Should I send this to yourself?' is better written, and more concise, as 'Should I send this to you?'

- Use the shift key – you need capital letters at the beginning of a sentence, for names and for proper nouns eg Mrs Smith, America, Monday

- 'They invited... Marnie and me' or 'Marnie and I'? The easy way to get this right is mentally to remove the words 'Marnie and' from the sentence. It then becomes either 'They invited me' or 'They invited I'. You know the first one sounds right, so then you can just add the missing words back into the sentence

# LAST WORDS

We hope you have enjoyed this pocketful of ideas on writing for business and feel confident to use our three phase approach to writing clearly and concisely. We're happy for you to contact us if you have more questions.

These are some of the books we have found useful and recommend to you for further study and insights.

**Ken and Kate Back**, *Assertiveness at Work*, McGraw-Hill (2005)

**Tony and Barry Buzan**, *The Mind Map Book*, BBC Active (2009)

**Robert Cialdini**, *Influence: Science and Practice*, Pearson (2008)

**Robert Gentle**, *Read This!: Business Writing that Works*, Prentice Hall (2001)

**John Kirkman and Christopher Turk**, *Effective Writing: Improving Scientific, Technical and Business Communication*, Taylor & Francis (1988)

**Bill McFarlan**, *Drop the Pink Elephant: 15 ways to say what you mean – and mean what you say*, Capstone (2004)

**Kay Sayce**, *What not to write: An A-Z of the Dos and Don'ts of Good English*, Words at Work (2006)

## About the Authors

**Stella Collins, BSc, MSc, FITOL**

Stella is a passionate advocate for enhanced communication skills.
With 16 years experience in the IT industry and 12 years in L&D, her
company, Stellar Learning, transforms training particularly if it's tough,
technical or tortuous. She founded The Brain Friendly Learning Group,
speaks regularly at conferences, has co-published six e-books and is
a regular writer for training publications as well as having her own
blog. She consults internationally on communication skills for SME and blue chip clients.
She loves helping people with writing to make life easier for both writers and readers.

**Beth Curl, BSc, MCIPD**

Beth believes in 'giving the best to and getting the best from people'.
From research chemist to founder of Hyproformance Ltd, she views
effective writing as a cornerstone to business success. Through 25
years as a management development consultant to organisations in the
private and public sectors, Beth has distilled out key principles for
communicating clearly in writing. Her goal is always to get the desired
response from the reader, whilst making the task of writing easier and
faster. She shares these concepts through workshops, coaching and
her blog.

# Pocketbooks – *available in both paperback and digital formats*

360 Degree Feedback
Absence Management
Appraisals
Assertiveness
Balance Sheet
Business Planning
Call Centre Customer Care
Career Transition
Coaching
Cognitive Behavioural Coaching
Communicator's
Competencies
Creative Manager's
C.R.M.
Cross-cultural Business
Customer Service
Decision-making
Delegation
Developing People
Discipline & Grievance
Diversity
Emotional Intelligence
Employment Law
Empowerment
Energy and Well-being
Facilitator's
Feedback

Flexible Workplace
Handling Complaints
Handling Resistance
Icebreakers
Impact & Presence
Improving Efficiency
Improving Profitability
Induction
Influencing
International Trade
Interviewer's
I.T. Trainer's
Key Account Manager's
Leadership
Learner's
Management Models
Manager's
Managing Assessment Centres
Managing Budgets
Managing Cashflow
Managing Change
Managing Customer Service
Managing Difficult Participants
Managing Recruitment
Managing Upwards
Managing Your Appraisal
Marketing

Meetings
Memory
Mentoring
Motivation
Negotiator's
Networking
NLP
Nurturing Innovation
Openers & Closers
People Manager's
Performance Management
Personal Success
Positive Mental Attitude
Presentations
Problem Behaviour
Problem Solving
Project Management
Psychometric Testing
Resolving Conflict
Reward
Sales Excellence
Salesperson's
Self-managed Development
Starting In Management
Storytelling
Strategy
Stress

Succeeding at Interviews
Tackling Difficult Conversations
Talent Management
Teambuilding Activities
Teamworking
Telephone Skills
Telesales
Thinker's
Time Management
Trainer's
Training Evaluation
Training Needs Analysis
Transfer of Learning
Virtual Teams
Vocal Skills
Working Relationships
Workplace Politics
Writing Skills

## Pocketfiles

Trainer's Blue Pocketfile of
Ready-to-use Activities

Trainer's Green Pocketfile of
Ready-to-use Activities

Trainer's Red Pocketfile of
Ready-to-use Activities

02.03.12